At the River's Edge

Meeting Jesus in Baptism

At the River's Edge
Meeting Jesus in Baptism

A·C·U
PRESS

Jeff W. Childers · Frederick D. Aquino

STUDY GUIDE BY

Jeanene Reese

AT THE RIVER'S EDGE:
Meeting Jesus in Baptism

The Heart of the Restoration
Special Supplement

A·C·U
PRESS

Acu Box 29138
Abilene, TX 79699
www.acu.edu/acupress

Study Guide · Jeanene Reese
Cover, document design & typesetting · William Rankin
This book is set in Adobe® Minion™ Pro 11.5/13, a font drawn by Robert Slimbach
and originally issued in 1990. This book was composed in Adobe® InDesign™.

ISBN 0-89112-033-5

¶ 5 4 3 2 1

Contents

Introduction

> Undergoing baptism implies that we are changing cultures.
> It reminds us of the seriousness of our decision to wear the
> name of Christ, to be his disciples. It celebrates the union
> of divine and human, not only in our Lord and savior, but
> in ever-increasing ways in our own lives as we serve the
> God who met us at the river's edge.

This rich picture and the text of this booklet are drawn
from the book, *Unveiling Glory: Visions of Christ's Transforming Presence,* by Jeff Childers and Fred Aquino. The
book's theme is that salvation in Christ Jesus is dominated
by the lifelong experience of being transformed into his
image. By gazing on the Lord's glory with unveiled faces
(2 Corinthians 3:18), we find ourselves being changed,
over time, to fit the picture we see in him. Chapter 3 of
the book focuses especially on Jesus' baptism and his call
to discipleship, a call so vivid and so compelling that we
chose to adapt that material for this brief study.

Baptism is often at the center of controversy among
believers. This booklet is not trying to answer all the
controversial questions. Many of the discussions about
baptism—for both those who stress baptism's importance
and for those who argue that it is unnecessary—are so
tied to modern agendas that they never seem to talk about
baptism the way the Apostles do, or to delve into the full
richness we find in Scripture. We believe that Christian
baptism is essential to the disciple's full participation in
the life of Jesus. We desire not only to proclaim strongly

the importance of baptism but also to deepen the reader's appreciation for the wonderful and unique ways that baptism shapes and empowers the Christian life.

Enriching our understanding of Christian baptism begins with a look at Jesus' own baptism in the Jordan. At the river's edge, we catch a glimpse of the Father, Son, and Spirit conversing together, sharing the life that is our birthright, too. By joining Jesus in the river, by answering his radical call to discipleship, we find ourselves immersed into a new world, one in which we learn to live according to the redemptive rhythm of death and new life.

These few pages do not attempt to explore every nuance of baptism nor anticipate every question. Their purpose is not to focus primarily on the external characteristics of baptism, however important, but rather to invite the reader into Jesus' own story and, thereby, to *be transformed*. To participate in Jesus' death and resurrection, after all, is to be changed utterly.

If you are a reader who has been baptized, this booklet is a call for deeper understanding, a challenge to lead the cross-shaped life begun in your baptism. If you have not been baptized, it is an invitation to come to the water where Jesus waits, to enter his story, to share his life, to walk with him to the cross, to be empowered by his resurrection.

Whether you are just considering baptism, are a new Christian, or a veteran believer, I invite you to share in Jesus' own baptism, his ministry, his suffering and death, and his glorious resurrection. I encourage you to come to the river where Jesus waits.

Jack R. Reese
Dean, Graduate School of Theology
Abilene Christian University

At the River's Edge:
Meeting Jesus in Baptism

> Baptism is designed to introduce the subjects of it into
> the participation of the blessings of the death and resur-
> rection of Christ.
>
> *Alexander Campbell (1866)*

*Many exciting things happened in the little church where
I grew up, but nothing captured our attention like an
impending baptism. Whether a long-planned event or
the spontaneous response to an inspiring sermon, a
public baptism was an event of great importance. The
preacher would announce the candidate's intent with
joyful solemnity. Then he took the confession of faith.
We all knew the words by rote, but we felt a comfortable
sense of satisfaction hearing them repeated once again.
It was part of a well-worn routine—more than routine;
the words and actions of the whole event seemed by their
familiar ceremony to involve us all in something deeper
than the moment, something extraordinary.*

*As the candidate and the one baptizing him withdrew
to get ready, men came forward to remove the pulpit that
was blocking our view. Someone would lead a few songs
or offer a meditation. He might fill the time with stirring
remembrances of the days when baptisms occurred in
rivers and ponds, or stock-tanks. Women bustled to check
on the facilities, helping female candidates get dressed and
ready for the water. While the pre-baptismal arrange-
ments progressed, the air was charged with expectation.*

Finally, as the pair went down into the water, children craned their necks to get a better look. They strained to catch every detail—partly in case they might witness a rare but memorable baptismal mishap, maybe even a capsizing. But they stared mostly because they knew instinctively that something special was underway. The very young understood little about what was happening, yet even they could sense the energy of the moment.

Then the person baptizing would lift a hand, invoke the names of Father, Son, and Spirit, and plunge the candidate beneath the water. After that, a transformation occurred. Something changed. We knew it had changed because people kept saying so. They quoted scripture to prove it. But there were other signs. For one, we immediately began singing the most cheerful songs of celebration. But also, once the person was dressed and among us again, he became a star. After the service, we would all press in around him, congratulating him, reveling in his celebrity status. He was special; what had just happened was special—for all of us. But most of all, if the baptism happened on a Sunday, as it often did, the transformation was signaled by his very first participation in the Lord's Supper. We would hold off serving it, delaying the whole service until he was dressed and ready. It was almost a meal prepared especially for him. He was a guest of the Lord's church, entitled to the first portion of his body. And from that time on, we would call him "Christian."

Jeff

The world is lost and broken, but God is fixing his world by unveiling himself in Jesus and drawing the world into that picture. As we peer into its glory, it captures us, involving our lives in its project, changing us into its own image and making us like Jesus (2 Corinthians 3:18). We know this because of our own experience as Jesus' disciples, beginning with our baptism. Baptism unveils a picture of the Lord. The waters of baptism show us a portrait of the Jesus who calls people to change their lives and become his disciples, accepting a total immersion into him and embarking on a lifelong journey of following in his footsteps.

In our churches, debates about the essentiality of baptism have been common—yet serious discussions of baptism's essence have been rare. Baptism is not just a command to be obeyed, an essential requirement to be checked off the list. Baptism is important because, in its essence, it connects the disciple to Jesus Christ. That is its basic meaning and the key to its significance. Discussing baptism's essentiality reveals little, but looking into its essence can open our eyes to see the power of Jesus to cleanse and renew broken lives, directing them towards a new purpose. To understand and celebrate the intimate connection we share with Jesus as his disciples, we start at the place where the ministry of Jesus and the life of Christian discipleship both begin: the baptism of Jesus.

Viewing Jesus from the Riverbank

The Jordan river may seem an unlikely place for a divine epiphany. Sublime scenes call for extraordinary settings, but if there was anything extraordinary about the place of Jesus' baptism, it was not obvious. The Jordan river was a useful place, but not a grand or extraordinary one—hardly a locale befitting divinity. It was a place to fill buckets and jars, a place to water animals, a place for washing clothes and scrubbing pans. As the Aramean general Naaman had observed long before, the waters of the Jordan were not the most appealing, a far cry from the clear mountain streams and sparkling springs you could find elsewhere. Yet it was onto this plain stage that the Son of God stepped, proceeding down into the muddy current that was the lifeblood of his homeland. The brown water swirled around his knees as the coarse sediment of the river bottom squished up between his toes.

The assortment of humanity gathered on Jordan's banks emphasized the unrefined earthiness of the scene. John the Baptist was there. He had the appearance of a desert rascal, a wild man living on the edge of civilization, whose lifestyle and sermons called into question the social conventions that most decent people took

5

for granted. To many, he would not have seemed fit to entertain royalty—except perhaps as a royal prisoner and victim.

Then there were the people who came to hear John. All kinds of people. Some were despised tax collectors, representing a sort of government-sanctioned banditry. They had plenty, but it would never occur to most of them to share even their spare tunics with the destitute. Soldiers were there too, the habitual extortionists of the poor, who bullied the weak for profit and sport. Even the religious leaders who came out to the river were exposed as hypocrites, proud of their heritage and religious devotion but devoid of genuine good fruit. Then there were the crowds of ordinary people, women and men and children of all sorts, some content, others in deep need, all of them moving within the rhythms of joy and grief that mark the fragile and uncertain days of human life.

At the Jordan, Jesus' humanity is clear to see. The atmosphere of the riverbank setting is saturated with the aroma of everything earthly and human, and to the casual observer, Jesus seemed to fit right in. Yet even within the spectacle of human frailty that we encounter in that Judean desert, we experience the full presence of God. Sinners were assembling at the riverside because they believed the Lord was up to something. These sad specimens of depravity and corruption were ready to practice repentance by confessing their sins, receiving baptism, and changing their lifestyles. By God's power, the muddy waters of Jordan were becoming a symbol of the divine purity that was capable of washing clean even the most filthy hearts. Repentance and transformation were clear signs of God's presence. God had not distanced himself from the world but was as deeply involved in it as ever. John confirmed this with his preaching, insist-

6   ing that God's ancient promises were on the move. The kingdom of heaven was near. The ragged man clothed in animal skins was a messenger, pointing to the work of God in their midst and preparing for the arrival of the Lord himself (Matthew 3:1–12; Luke 3:1–20).

Then he came. As a man, in the water, surrendering himself into the hands of a fellow man, he came to be baptized. Yet for all his humanity, the divine presence in this scene is overwhelming, not only in the riverbank atmosphere, but in the event itself. By the time it was all over, Jesus was drenched from head to toe, lanky strands of hair pasted to his glistening forehead. In a small and desolate part of the world, far away and long ago, a carpenter's son was baptized. Yet the infinite expanse of heaven opened and the voice of the Eternal One spoke over him, confirming that he was the obedient Son who was well pleasing to his heavenly Father, while the Spirit of God passed between them both, conveying divine love and power. A small event—but of cosmic significance.

Matthew, Mark, and Luke each present Jesus' baptism as a pivotal moment in his life and ministry, a key to understanding who he is (Matthew 3:13–17; Mark 1:9–11; Luke 3:21–22). In John's Gospel, the Baptist describes it as a moment of divine testimony to Jesus' identity (John 1:31–34). By his own admission, Jesus was baptized "to fulfill all righteousness." It was the right thing for him to do. Though people have argued about the precise reasons Jesus underwent baptism, the picture we get at the Jordan is unmistakable. At the river is a picture of God's fullness in his activity as divine Father, Son, and Spirit, embracing one another in an unspeakably intimate relationship. We see the full Jesus, human and divine. As in his birth, in his baptism the Messiah is "God with us," unveiling for us a vision of divinity and humanity working together.

> "The Trinity is an attempt to affirm that God is a thoroughly relational being. The doctrine of the Trinity accents this truth by claiming that God not only forms relationships but that He is a relationship."
>
> C. Leonard Allen & Danny G. Swick (2001)

Jesus' baptism marks the beginning point of his ministry, but even more, it shows us what he is calling us to. He's inviting us to share with him in the whole life of God—Father, Son, and Spirit, entering an intimate

7

relationship with the Lord by allowing ourselves to be immersed fully into Christ and embarking on an adventure of radical discipleship. Like the incarnation itself, baptism presents a full picture, holding together many diverse pieces that seem nearly incompatible yet are reconciled in Christ. The call to a holiness that makes us distinct from the world is here joined to a call to ministry that irrevocably connects us to it, all under the auspices of Christ's invitation to wade with him into the waters. And in order to understand fully what is involved in this call to discipleship, we need to explore the significance of our own riverbank scene, the moment in which we join Jesus in baptism.

Christian Baptism: Stepping into the Picture

Christian baptism enacts the very meaning of salvation, because it instigates and celebrates a connection with Jesus Christ. When a person is baptized "in the name of Jesus" to receive "the gift of the Spirit" (Acts 2:38), he or she is putting on Jesus, like putting on a different suit of clothes or a new skin (Galatians 3:27). This is why early Christians often decorated their baptistries with the scene of Jesus' baptism in the Jordan, depicting with paint and mosaic tile their belief that the person stepping down into the water for baptism was joining Jesus there. He or she was stepping into the gospel story, merging into the picture of the gospel that is unveiled in Christ.

Baptism and the Drama of Salvation

Early Christians saw connections between the waters of baptism and key moments in history:

- Creation (Genesis 1:2; John 3:5–8; Titus 3:5; 2 Corinthians 5:17)

- Salvation from the Flood (Genesis 6–8; 1 Peter 3:20–21)

- Crossing the Red Sea at the Exodus (Exodus 14:21; 1 Corinthians 10:1–2, 6)

In each instance, water represents life and salvation—yet it is also a dangerous force that can be faced only by faith in the power of God to transform its deadliness into redemption.

8

Jesus' baptism not only marks the beginning point of his ministry; it also teaches us what discipleship looks like and actually puts us into the picture of God's saving work. In baptism, we're stepping into the gospel landscape at some of its most prominent points:

First, we're reborn by water and the Spirit, experiencing a "washing of rebirth and renewal," as a new creation cleansed of sin (John 3:5–8; Titus 3:5; 2 Corinthians 5:17)—all because God entered the world as a newborn baby when the same Spirit descended on a young girl named Mary. Our baptism connects us to the birth of Jesus. It is as if the Spirit of God were hovering over the waters, ready to bring forth a new creation at God's command (Genesis 1:2). We put on the "new self, which is being renewed in knowledge according to the image of its creator" (Colossians 3:10).

> **Salvation as New Creation**
>
> "I will give you a new heart and put a new spirit in you...."
>
> *Ezekiel 36:26*
>
> "Neither circumcision nor uncircumcision means anything; what counts is a new creation."
>
> *Galatians 6:15*
>
> "Christianity is very far from being a mere redemption from sin, or salvation from punishment, or selfish rewards for obedience. It designs not only to bestow remission of sins but to effect a renovation—a regeneration of the soul. Indeed, it is not too much to affirm that it can be a means of salvation only as it is a means of renovation...."
>
> *Robert Richardson (c. 1847)*

Second, in the water, we're also joining Jesus in the Jordan river. His presence in the water purifies it, transforming it from a muddy stream into the cleansing waters that sanctify us to become his servants. We come up out of the water as disciples, listening to his teaching and following him as he goes about in the world helping people and proclaiming the gospel. Long after we've dried ourselves off, we continue to learn from him, fleshing out our baptismal commitment by remaining loyal to him, going wherever he leads us, growing in faith and maturity, and following his example.

Third, taken under the water, we also join Jesus in the tomb, meeting him in his death and entering into his resurrection (Romans 6:3-4). Baptism is death and life, burial and resurrection—a turning point and a fresh start. Connected intimately with the Lord in baptism, we learn to fulfill our baptism by dying to ourselves and "presenting [our] bodies as a living sacrifice" (Romans 12:2). Rising up out of the waters, we are awakened from a deadly slumber to walk in the fresh daylight of a new morning (Ephesians 5:14).

In short, our baptism paints us into the central portrait of God's salvation—the life, death, and resurrection of Jesus. It lands us squarely in the middle of the gospel action so that the Jesus story becomes our story. This is the essence of baptism and ought to be the gist of our teaching about it. Baptism is a marvelous point of entry for disciples and should not be commandeered by agendas that reduce it to a simple rule or that focus solely on debates about its essentiality. Such agendas distract us from the essence of baptism, weakening our understanding of the discipleship it pictures.

A Picture of Collaboration

Churches of Christ are famous for discussing—and debating—baptism. In sermons, books, pamphlets, magazines, and lectureships, we have taken on a multitude of questions about the nature, function, and mode of baptism. Is it essential to salvation? How should we do it—and does that matter? Who needs it—and at what age or level of understanding? The questions are potentially endless, and it's unlikely that total agreement on every baptismal issue can ever be achieved. Yet often such questions drive a wedge between elements of discipleship that should never be separated.

10   For example, when we ask, "Is baptism the work of God or a human work?" we are forcing a false distinction that does not fit the full incarnational glory of God being unveiled in Christ. Like salvation and the Christian life, baptism is neither solely God's work nor solely ours. Sal-

vation is a free gift of God, to be sure, yet the manner in which we experience it entails a response of gratitude and the full investment of our own efforts. When we are thrust under the water, we surrender control of our bodies to the one baptizing us, and we surrender control of our lives

> "No doubt the gospel is quite free, as free as the Victoria Cross, which anyone can have who is prepared to face the risks; but it means time, and pains, and concentrating all one's energies upon a mighty project. You will not stroll into Christlikeness with your hands in your pockets, shoving the door open with a careless shoulder. This ·is no hobby for one's leisure moments...."
>
> *A. J. Gossip (1924)*

into the hands of the one who saves us. We confess our inadequacies, accepting the unmerited gift and work of God and recognizing the sufficiency of the incarnation, the cross, and the resurrection (Romans 5:1–2; Ephesians 2:8–9). Yet we stand there in the water because of our own decision, and the words—and sins—that we confess are our own. We rise up out of the water to become God's partners, not his puppets, putting all our efforts into the pursuit of a new lifestyle (Romans 6:1–4, 12–14).

Baptism recognizes and conveys the picture of collaboration that has been a part of God's design for his creation from the beginning. It invites us to trust God, each day falling back into the arms of the only one who can support and save us. Yet it also invites us to reverse the evasive, finger-pointing tendencies that we learned from Adam and Eve by taking full responsibility for ourselves and recognizing that the effectiveness of Christian living depends a great deal on the strength of our commitments and our own hard work as God's new creatures. Is baptism a human work or a divine one? The question itself pits humanity against God, physical against spiritual, and external against internal. It breaks the mystical union of divine and human that we see in Jesus. Salvation in Christ and discipleship combine these things, however, just like baptism does.

Church leaders need to liberate discussions about baptism from such false dichotomies. The way we talk about and

11

> "Baptism is no human trifle, but instituted by God Himself.... It is of the greatest importance that we esteem Baptism excellent, glorious, and exalted, for which we contend and fight chiefly, because the world is now so full of sects clamoring that Baptism is an external thing, and that external things are of no benefit."
>
> *Martin Luther (1530)*

> "*All the means of salvation are means of enjoyment, not of procurement*.... No one is to be put under the water of regeneration for the purpose of procuring life, but for the purpose of enjoying the life of which he is possessed."
>
> *Alexander Campbell (1866)*

practice baptism ought to remind us that there is a real connection between the work of Christ and the Christian life. The Christian life reflects an ongoing transformation into the likeness of God through the Spirit, and it is by our identification with Christ that the image is renewed. Baptism initiates us into the new humanity by connecting us with the Second Adam. It is not primarily an act of obedience that qualifies us for salvation. It is not like a lever we throw to receive the membership card that will gain us entry at the pearly gates. Nor is it a mere external human work, to be downplayed due to an emphasis on God's grace or to be superseded by an emphasis on a person's internal conversion experience. The picture we get at the baptistry should match the one we get at the Jordan, where the fragments of our humanity are being put back together under God, not broken further apart.

A Picture of Growth

Baptism also reminds us that discipleship is both a one-time commitment to Christ and an ongoing journey with him. Churches of Christ have tended to look at salvation through the window of conversion, emphasizing salvation as an object we come to possess or a situation we enjoy—it is forgiveness of sins, a legal status of guiltlessness before God, or a blanket transfer of membership from "world" to "church." Salvation is all these things, but it is also so much more. Unfortunately, by focusing on the legal and static dimensions of salvation, we've handicapped our ability to appreciate baptism's power to shape all of life.

It's true that baptism pictures discipleship as a moment of decision, a one-time act of obedience and dedication to Christ, perhaps the culmination of a long process of thinking and studying. Once immersed, we have "crossed over from death to life" (1 John 3:14); we belong to Christ and become one of the saved, all the way, all at once. It is a crucial moment, worth all the attention and fanfare we can give it, a bright day that we mark forever on our calendars and look back on fondly. When parents and church leaders strive to find the most effective ways of bringing people to the point of decision, their energies are not misdirected. In fact, most congregations should work even harder to explore creative ways of investing their church's practice of baptism with its full meaning and of amplifying the excitement surrounding this wonderful rite of passage. Baptism is a unique celebration crowning a person's final commitment to Christ.

The Meaning of Baptism

Some ways churches today are exploring the depths of baptism:

- Planning sermon and class series on: the different meanings of baptism; biblical images connected with baptism; connections between baptism and different phases or experiences of life

- Encouraging public baptisms and emphasizing baptism's communal witness and celebration

- Planning the structure of Sunday worship around baptismal events; involving the person baptized in the planning

- Having a church-wide feast following a baptism

- Reading and discussing some of the many fine spiritual meditations written about baptism over the centuries

- Composing special songs for baptismal events

- Recovering balanced curriculum aimed specifically at preparing youth for baptism and discipleship

- Encouraging family celebrations of baptismal birthdays

- Having the church gather around after a baptism to offer specific blessings or personal services

- Clothing the person baptized in a new outfit picked out for the occasion

13

Yet baptism also pictures that once-for-all moment as a starting point, the induction into a continuous process of "being saved" (1 Corinthians 1:18). We're accepting the call to follow Jesus every day. By being united with him in his resurrection, we start a journey towards a final destination that is a lifetime away—being conformed to the image of Christ. As a symbol of new birth, baptism directs the church to emphasize the importance of Christian growth. It's therefore not enough to get our children and converts baptized. We bring them to the riverbank, but we also wait for them on the other side, ready to walk alongside them, telling them stories of the kingdom, challenging them to grow, and providing the resources they need to mature and to serve their Lord. Being preoccupied only with baptism as the culmination of salvation can cause us to neglect the importance of providing for Christian growth. Pre-baptismal instruction should take its cue from Jesus' teaching, focusing more on the demands of discipleship, the meaning of baptism for a person's lifestyle, than on the singular goal of getting him or her into the baptistry. The education of new disciples needs to include training in the habits that will cultivate the continuing formation of their knowledge, character, and abilities to serve. Baptized into Christ, disciples ought to find themselves in a body that helps them grow, one devoted to the practices of gazing on Jesus so fixedly that transformation happens naturally.

However, if we treat salvation only as a tidy, wrapped package delivered at baptism, we won't know what to make of growth when it occurs. At baptism, the disciple may "know enough," but it won't be enough for long. Over time, disciples learn more, and they change in remarkable ways, sometimes gradually, sometimes in great leaps. Throughout our lives, there will be times when we come to see our Lord and our discipleship in such fundamentally different ways as to make our earlier understandings seem obsolete and childish. This is all natural. Jesus' first disciples revised their understandings of him as they went along. This did not invalidate their original faith,

14

though, nor did it prompt them to seek rebaptism. Reaching new levels of understanding and commitment was a normal part of the discipleship experience. Paul saw his life as an adventure of constant progress towards the goal of fully knowing Jesus (Philippians 3:10–14).

New disciples should be taught to expect and welcome seasons of growth. For their part, older disciples show their maturity when they recognize that they also are works in progress. They know their limitations. They listen to others humbly because they've learned that there is always more to learn. They know that not all change is growth, yet they also realize that there is no growth without change. The thought of adjusting their beliefs, accepting new practices, or correcting their understanding of some passage of scripture does not frighten them. They have learned to walk each day in the freshness of their baptism, living at the horizons of their own experience as they are being transformed daily into the image of the Lord. They're mature enough to be at peace in their relationship with Jesus, wise enough to know that he is always calling them forward.

To sum up, the multi-faceted picture we see in Jesus' baptism is reflected in our own baptisms and in the Christian life: salvation is a possession, but it is also a process; baptism is a destination, but it is also a point of departure; it is God's divine work, but it also involves our human efforts. The Christian life, just like the life and work of Jesus, has various aspects. The danger is in allowing ourselves to be so mesmerized by one of these facets that we neglect, or even reject, others that are equally indispensable. Guarding against this trap is one of the principal reasons for coming back to the full picture of Jesus over and over again. The total image of Christ that is being unveiled to us cannot be reduced to any one fragment. The claim that he lays on us as his disciples is just as absolute. Baptism presents us with a picture of what it means to live within these tensions, and we thereby mirror his image in discipleship, for discipleship swallows up a person's whole life into Jesus as surely as the waters of baptism swallow up her whole body.

15

A Deadly Vision

"Can you be baptized with the baptism I am baptized with?" Jesus asked his disciples, referring to his death. "You will be," he insisted (Mark 10:38–39). The Jesus pictured in children's Bibles is a safe and welcoming figure, the sort of person who smiles a lot and tousles kids' hair. They sit on his lap as he tells them he loves them, as if to say that following him will be a warm and cozy experience, making for a happy life on earth. This picture isn't fake—so long as it's not the only picture one has. Jesus is also the terrifying Lord of judgment pictured in Revelation 1 and the stern critic of the Gospel texts, who accuses even his closest followers of being people of little faith who are stubbornly hard-hearted. The full picture of Christ reminds us that his call to join him in baptism has a hard edge. Jesus desires to have a close personal relationship with each of us, but he insists that the intimacy can be genuine only after we've made some hard decisions and major sacrifices.

With a marvelous upside-down flair, Jesus captures the essence of this new life by depicting it as death: "if anyone would come after me, he must deny himself and take up his cross and follow me" (Matthew 16:24). Following Jesus means shouldering a cross and treading a grim path to a certain death (Luke 14:25–35). The path of discipleship is like the journey of a death-row victim walking the long mile to his or her own execution. That walk has a way of putting things into perspective. What used to be so captivating—getting more money, building a larger home, settling petty grievances, impressing people, advancing career status—hardly seems important any more, because disciples carry their own deaths

"He will be the Truth that will offend them one and all,
a stone that makes men stumble and a rock that makes them fall.
Many will be broken so that He can make them whole;
many will be crushed and lose their own soul."

Michael Card (1985)

around with them, and the ordeal gives them a drastically different vision of reality. As Dietrich Bonhoeffer said, "When Christ calls a man, he bids him come and die."

There is no legitimate way to domesticate Christ's call. In order to find your life, you must lose it (Mark 8:35). Despite the tenets of some popular versions of Christianity, discipleship is not simply another item you can build into your portfolio of activities, like Little League, school programs, and camping trips. It allows no competition. Some people hope to find in Jesus that "little something special" they need in order to round out their lives, but Jesus is not just another product that people can drop into their shopping carts. Jesus said, "if anyone comes to me and does not hate his father and mother, his wife and children…yes, even his own life—he cannot be my disciple" (Luke 14:26). Entering the kingdom is an all-or-nothing venture. It's not like joining a club or watching a football game from the stands. Nor is it a simple matter of adopting a body of teachings or quaint religious practices—what many think of as "joining a church." To become a disciple is to move from one world to another—to emigrate from a false world of shadows and lies to the world of God's original intent.

After his baptism, Jesus started his ministry, inviting people to step into that picture of fellowship with God that we're privileged to see from the banks of the Jordan. Even after his resurrection, Jesus' apostles continued to welcome others into the picture by making disciples all over the world, "baptizing them in the name of the Father and of the Son and of the Holy Spirit" (Matthew 28:19). Like Jesus and his apostles, we should be excited about inviting people to join us as Jesus' followers. However, also like them, we need to be up front about the cost of discipleship. Church leaders should resist the temptation to pull punches for the sake of attracting more customers or to emphasize free grace.

17

Churches that focus on God's grace in salvation and on Jesus' open reception of sinners sometimes get into the habit of glossing over the high standards and rigorous demands of discipleship. The fact is, following Jesus isn't for everyone. It is only for those willing to give up everything. Against the instincts of our consumer-oriented society, a fair presentation of the gospel message doesn't just try to entice people with all the things Jesus will do for them; it illuminates what Jesus is calling them to be. Jesus holds a winnowing fork in his hands. The hard edge of his message is like sharp tines, shaking out the chaff from the good grain (Luke 3:17).

Grace & Discipleship

"Cheap grace is the preaching of forgiveness without requiring repentance, baptism without church discipline, Communion without confession, absolution without personal confession. Cheap grace is grace without discipleship, grace without the cross, grace without Jesus Christ, living and incarnate.

Costly grace is the treasure hidden in the field; for the sake of it a person will gladly go and sell all he has.... It is the kingly rule of Christ, for whose sake a person will pluck out the eye which causes him to stumble.... It is costly because it costs a person his life and it is grace because it gives a person the only true life.... What has cost God so much cannot be cheap for us."

Dietrich Bonhoeffer (1937)

Jesus does not invite people to accept the gospel because they will find it fulfilling or enjoyable, nor even just because it will be good for them and their families—though it may turn out to be all these things. Jesus invites them to lose their lives for him, to join a fellowship where they will be expected "to serve, not to be served" (Matthew 20:28). Our evangelistic efforts should make these costs clear.

The Jesus who draws all people to himself is a man who has been lifted up on the cross, and it is in the display of this image that the world glimpses the antidote to the poison that is killing it (John 3:14–15; 12:32). "Whoever wants to save his life will lose it, but whoever loses his life for me will save it" (Luke 9:24). Discipleship that begins with baptism and holds the image of Jesus as its inspiration is driven by the dynamic to surrender, to find life in death, to serve and to sacrifice—not to be served. When we draw people into our fellowship under the pretense that Christianity is all about being served and feeling satisfied, we create a momentum in the wrong direction, one that can be very difficult to redirect and that leads people away from the true picture of a Jesus who wades humbly into the water. Such false images create communities enslaved to self-serving motives.

But we who are seeking Christ in his fullness are continuously reminded that we are buried with Jesus in baptism. Putting faith in Christ requires accepting the full implications of that death. It is not a matter of placing Jesus' name at the top of an old list, but of throwing away the list altogether and receiving a new one, where Jesus is the only item and where his kingdom is the only agenda, the only reality:

> "No one can serve two masters" (Matthew 6:24).

> "No one who puts his hand to the plow and looks back is fit for service in the kingdom of God" (Luke 9:62).

> "Any of you who does not give up everything she has cannot be my disciple" (Luke 14:33).

These are hard sayings. Before the Master Builder constructs a new luxury home on the property of our lives, the site must be cleared and leveled, the ruins of the dilapidated and condemned old building removed and thrown away. The opportunity is a marvelous one; the kingdom of heaven is like a hidden treasure, easily worth the investment of everything we possess. But it does cost everything. Just as Jesus' own baptism holds together many tensions, Christian baptism simultaneously plunges the disciple into the termination of one life and the creation of a new one. These rhythms of death-and-life draw us into Jesus' own practices and cause us to share in his miraculous identity.

The Shape of Christian Spirituality

"When we enter into the waters of baptism, we enter into a divine connection with the suffering of Jesus and with his resurrection. We are brought into a pattern of life that is an actual identification with Jesus. Baptism is therefore not only an identification with Christ but a calling to live the baptized life. The calling which baptism symbolizes gives concrete form to our spirituality...."

Robert E. Webber (1999)

19

Practicing the Death & Life of Baptism

The death that comes with discipleship is difficult, but it is also liberating. It rejects one world for the sake of affirming a better one, a world where we enjoy freedoms that the old world can never know. For example, the death we experience in discipleship liberates us to be more generous with our possessions. Like the stingy person who demonstrates uncharacteristically charitable attitudes when preparing his final will, Christians who have died so that their "life is now hidden with Christ in God" (Colossians 3:3) will not hesitate to dig deep into their pockets to help others. They feel only a loose attachment to the cars they drive, the houses they use, and the bank accounts they manage. Losing them would be no real loss; giving them up is a comparatively trivial matter. Viewing their possessions from within the tomb of baptism, they find it easier to take the risks that come with sharing sacrificially. Out of their sacrifice comes new hope for those in need.

The dead in Christ can also be more lavish with their forgiveness. They can relinquish their grudges against each other and lay aside their differences. By focusing on their common life in Christ, they learn not to be distracted by the peripheral matters that are usually at the root of interpersonal conflicts and church division. Keeping unveiled eyes locked on Jesus, the glory they behold transforms their vision so that most of what people argue about appears uninteresting. By accepting Jesus' call, they've signed on to an agenda more grand than anything church fights offer, an agenda so rewarding that they're willing to make personal sacrifices in order to stay on track. Wherever Christians are in the habit of fighting with one another, they show that they have lost sight of their true calling and have forgotten whose servants they are (Romans 14:4). They have not learned to keep practicing the self-denial of their baptism, having forgotten the principle that death to self is usually just the thing needed to breathe new life into a relationship.

The disciple's passage to death in baptism also becomes the doorway to vibrant congregational ministry. When people surrender fully to the Lord, they exhibit new levels of commitment and become more willing, like Jesus, to brave risks for the sake of the kingdom. We value what we've invested in. Having committed everything to the Lord's kingdom vision, we discover that other activities don't matter

> "A community is only a community when the majority of its members is making the transition from 'the community for myself' to 'myself for the community,' when each person's heart is opening to all the others.... This is the movement from egoism to love, from death to resurrection...."
>
> *Jean Vanier (1979)*

so much. We find life and significance in our involvement in the church's mission. And rather than griping that the church doesn't meet some need of ours, we follow the path of Christ by expending our energies serving and helping others. Rather than focusing on what we get out of the church, we're preoccupied with discovering what we can put into it.

These are all ways in which the death we experience in baptism is really life. The water of baptism conveys this message. Water is precious to us because we need it to live, but it also frightens us, because a person can drown in it. In the same way, baptism presents us with a difficult picture. The deep joy and full life to which Jesus calls us seem to be in tension with the grim chore of carrying a cross. It's tempting to turn loose of the challenging side in order to embrace something warm and comfortable. But to do so is to corrupt the very

> Without our suffering, our work would just be social work, very good and helpful, but not the work of Jesus Christ, not part of the Redemption. Jesus wanted to help by sharing our life, our loneliness, our agony, our death. Only by being one with us has he redeemed us. We are asked to do the same.
>
> *Mother Theresa (1975)*

meaning of baptism, muddying its beauty and power.

Over the centuries, many people—and even churches— have tried to re-mold Jesus into a shape easier to manage and more compatible with their own programs, hoping to

pass off a poorly forged portrait of Jesus as the real thing.
Wherever the teaching of Jesus becomes uncomfortable,
they learn to ignore it, devising ways to sidestep his plain
demands or substituting their own hobbies for the items
he was truly passionate about. Not everyone claiming to
follow Jesus really does so (Matthew 7:21–23). Yet when
enough people agree together on a counterfeit definition
of discipleship, the image they present can be deceptively
compelling. A whole church can buy into a forgery.

We need to remain aware that a tendency lurks within
us to soften his claim on our lives. As he did with his first
disciples, Jesus calls us to be completely attentive to him.
And, like them, we must learn that what he often speaks
to us are stinging rebukes and demanding instructions. Yet
he has the heart of his Father, and even his harshest chal-
lenges are meant to be redemptive, rescuing us from our
own self-destructive ways. Discipleship may be as severe
as death, but for Jesus' followers, it is the only way to live.
Baptism captures the severity of this death, just as surely
as it involves us in the power of Jesus' resurrected life.

"Raised with Jesus…"

Christians identify with Jesus' resurrection both because
he is the first-fruits of the final resurrection for which
we all hope and because the power of the resurrection
is working in us now. "If anyone is in Christ, he is a new
creation" (2 Corinthians 5:17). Baptism pictures this
renewing and life-changing power at work. It forms
special connections to Jesus, involving the disciple in
Jesus' life and experience. Rising up out of the waters
of baptism, the Christian discovers that the same Spirit
that accomplished Jesus' victory over death has taken up
residence within, imparting new life to her own spirit
and bestowing the pledge of the final resurrection of her
body (Romans 8:10–11).

As Paul repeatedly stresses, it is the believers' participation "in Jesus Christ" that saves them. The resurrection
shows us what that participation looks like. Disciples

arise from the waters of baptism to begin a new life, the
Spirit-empowered journey towards Christlikeness. The
"mystery" of God's plan has finally been revealed, set in
motion by Jesus' resurrection. God established Jesus as
Lord. Having risen from the dead and ascended to his
Father, he sits at the right hand of God, enthroned over
the universe (Matthew 28:18). Everything is now moving
towards a single goal. When the times have been fulfilled,
everything will fit snugly under the lordship of Christ
(Ephesians 1:9–10). This is the Holy Spirit's principal
work in the world.

We see the Spirit's best work in this regard within the
Christian life. The
Spirit works to trans-
form character and
lifestyle so that the
disciple is a picture
of Jesus, exhibiting
the fruit of the Spirit's
presence (Galatians
5:16–26). The Spirit
brings the resurrected
Christ into the life of

> "We are buried with him in the element of water that we may rise again renewed by the Spirit. For in the water is the representation of death, in the Spirit is the pledge of life, that the body of sin may die through the water, which encloses the body as it were in a kind of tomb, that we, by the power of the Spirit, may be renewed from the death of sin being born again in God."
>
> *Ambrose of Milan (381)*

the believer. Having died to sin, disciples discover what
it means to be united with Jesus in his resurrection—it
means an opportunity to offer the parts of their bodies to
God, "as those who have been brought from death to life,"
to be living sacrifices, transformed through the renewal
of their minds (Romans 6:5, 13; 12:1–2). To confess Jesus
as Lord is not merely to claim a relationship with him;
it is to surrender to a very specific aim—being shaped
according to Jesus' image. Transformation into the image
of Christ is the chief aim of the Christian life, and it is
growing maturity in Christlikeness that validates authen-
tic Christian experience.

One of the church's most profound testimonies to
Jesus' resurrection is public baptism. By administering
baptism, the church professes the full gospel story in
a single act. Just as Jesus was the passive recipient of

resurrection power, so the candidate passively submits to being baptized and raised up into Christ to enjoy God's victory over the forces of evil. Yet the connection is not a vertical one only, for in baptism a person is also joined to the body of Jesus (1 Corinthians 12:13). When the members of a church gather around to witness the baptism, they rejoice since the person being baptized depicts what they themselves have become—integral members of Jesus' resurrected body. And ever after in life, we can call ourselves back to Christ, reclaiming the comfort and calling of our salvation by remembering, as Martin Luther put it, "I am baptized."

> "We must think of the post-resurrection body of Christ as a new kind of body because, in Paul's theology, the body of Christ incorporates an entire community of members through their baptism into his death and resurrection."
>
> *Carl Braaten* (2001)

A church that is baptizing is witnessing to the resurrection story as powerfully as the closing chapters of the Gospels do—and even more tangibly. Yet the church's most spectacular display of resurrection power occurs when the picture that baptism captures becomes a living reality in its midst, when it cooperates with the Spirit in the work of forming Christ in its members and in being Christ wherever it is. More than any historical evidences or logical argumentation, the transformation of Jesus' misguided and bickering early disciples into a potent and unified force for carrying out God's ministry of reconciliation in the world was the most striking evidence for the truth of the resurrection. And so it is today. By faith, the church has certain knowledge of the event of Jesus' resurrection. Yet it is by the dynamic evidence of resurrection power at work in its midst that the church engenders faith in others.

The church's compelling testimony to the resurrection is the display of ongoing transformation in the lives of its people, as they seek to live as disciples of Jesus whose daily lives are conforming to the baptismal rhythm of death and life.

Conclusion: The Benefits of Mutual Commitment

Baptism is not the sort of thing that comes naturally. It's an unusual spectacle. We all take baths, but this is different. Baptism involves rituals and words and a background story that only make sense within the Christian worldview and nowhere else. The ceremony, like the life it pictures, is nonsense to outsiders. What is life to us seems to them like death. Undergoing baptism implies that we are changing cultures. It reminds us of the

> **Buried with Christ in Baptism**
>
> "Christ's burial is more clearly represented by immersion: wherefore this manner of baptizing is more frequently in use and more commendable."
>
> *Thomas Aquinas (c. 1265)*

seriousness of our decision to wear the name of Christ, to be his disciples. It celebrates the union of divine and human, not only in our Lord and savior, but in ever-increasing ways in our own lives as we serve the God who met us at the river's edge.

Discipleship is an experience of following Jesus with an extreme level of commitment, being immersed into him, living within him as if he were the very environment of our lives, whatever the cost or stigma. This utter commitment to him is the foundation of much that disciples must be and do in order to reflect the Lord's glory. Yet the wonderful thing about discipleship is that the radical commitment works both ways. The Lord is just as devoted to us as he wants us to be towards him—even more so. God loved us enough to send his Son, who faced rejection and death, yet he came anyway. Even Jesus' most dedicated followers repeatedly misunderstood him, willfully disobeyed him, and ultimately abandoned him to the cross. Yet Jesus was merciful and faithful, keeping up his end of the relationship. Some of them followed him only because they hoped he would defeat the Romans. Others sought personal glory by requesting privileged status in the kingdom. Peter was so off-base at one point that Jesus

AT THE RIVER'S EDGE

identified him with Satan. Even in his darkest hour, Jesus' closest friends drifted off to sleep rather than keeping a supportive vigil at Gethsemane. Yet Jesus remained devoted to them.

Utter commitment to Jesus is not easy. It involves sacrifice. Like his first disciples, we fail and we fall down. We misunderstand and we get it wrong sometimes. We try to be like clean reflective lenses, showing the Lord's glory in our efforts to gaze only upon him, yet we often behave in ways that chip and scratch the surface of our lives so that the image we present is flawed and blurred. Sometimes we turn away to focus on something else altogether, losing the picture completely for awhile. The great comfort of radical discipleship is that it happens in an atmosphere of extreme love. Discipleship is not one-sided. It does not begin with us. Discipleship begins with the Lord. It is a response to the commitment God has already made to us, founded on a relationship and a covenant established in a muddy river in a tiny country where one who is both God and man humbled himself in the waters of baptism.

Study Guide

This study guide has two main sections. The first section begins with questions for deeper reflection and prayer that can be used by individuals to enhance personal insight or by groups in various settings to improve sharing and discussion. Their purpose is to draw each person more deeply into reflection and prayer about God's work in our lives. After the questions for reflection and prayer are questions appropriate for analysis and discussion. These may be used in combination with the reflection and prayer questions or by themselves.

The second section of this study guide includes two scenarios that offer readers an opportunity to explore the implications of *At the River's Edge* in true-to-life situations. After each scenario, discussion questions are included to assist in probing the issues presented.

However you use the study guide, it is intended to enhance your understanding of who God is, what he wants in our lives, and how he intends for us to live together. May you be blessed as you meet him at the river's edge.

Discussion Questions

For Reflection & Prayer

1 Read the account of Jesus' baptism in Matthew 3:13–17. Reflect on the ways that we see God as Father, Son

and Spirit in this picture. Of the three, which have you tended to associate with baptism most? What makes this significant to you and where you are in your life?

2 The authors suggest that the key to the significance of baptism is that it connects the disciple to Jesus Christ. Examine each of the following images of baptism. Meditate on what you find compelling about each one and why it is important to godly life. Select the image that is most meaningful in your life at this time and spend time in prayer about it: a · Baptism is a *beginning*—it gives us new direction in the journey we are taking, and a companion to journey with us; b · Baptism is a *birth*—it gives us new life, we are a new creation made perfect and pure; c · Baptism is a *bath*—it washes away our sins at once yet also continually makes us clean; d · Baptism is a *burial*—it calls us to die to ourselves and be raised again with Christ; e · Baptism is a *bond*—it provides us with a new identity, a new family, and the gift of the Spirit to hold it all together.

3 Reflect on the authors' statement, "The death that comes with discipleship is difficult, but it is also liberating" (p. 20). How have you experienced liberation in your walk with Jesus? What do you still need to put to death as a disciple?

4 Choose one of the following to reflect and pray about: a · If you are a baptized believer, how would your Christian life be the same or different if you focused each day on the freshness of your baptism and the promise of continual transformation into the image of the Lord? How is this the same or different than you have been living? b · If you are a seeker of God, how would your life be the same or different if you chose to respond to the Lord in baptism? What do you think needs transforming in your life? How would this decision impact the way you are living?

For Study & Analysis

1 Jesus' ministry and our Christian discipleship share the same beginning point: his baptism. How is that significant to you? Briefly share your baptismal story and what you treasure most about it.

2 How does knowing that baptism requires our collaboration with God affect your view of it? What significance does this insight have for your own life of faith?

3 Looking at the box "The Meaning of Baptism" on page 13, answer the following questions: In what ways can your church enhance an individual's preparation for baptism? How can you maximize the baptismal event? What can your congregation do better to journey with the newly baptized in their faith walk?

4 Examine each of the following demands Jesus makes. Choose one that is most appealing to you and explain why. Next, select one that is especially challenging and describe why. Finally share what the community of faith could do to help you better incorporate this discipleship principle into your faith walk: a · Denying self, taking up my cross and following Jesus (Matthew 16:28); b · Finding life by losing it (Luke 9:24); c · Hating father, mother, wife and children, even your own life (Luke 14:26); d · Serving instead of being served (Mt. 20:28); e · Giving up everything (Luke 14:33); f · Going into the world to make disciples (Matthew 28:19).

5 How is the gift of the Holy Spirit that you received at baptism an ongoing witness of God's promise in your life? What does it mean to be filled with the indwelling Spirit?

6 What is the true aim of Christian discipleship? What does the resurrection have to do with it? How will you know if you are achieving this aim in your life? in your church?

29

Scenarios

Scenario 1: "Help Me, Lord"

The Situation

Charles Gibson closed his Bible, finished scribbling some notes, took off his glasses, and sat back with a smile. He was almost ready for an important conversation with his fourteen-year-old grandson, Adam. He just needed some quiet time for reflection and prayer.

It seemed like only yesterday that the family had celebrated Adam's arrival as the first grandchild. "Where had the time gone?" wondered Charles. "It's hard to believe that the boy's already in his teens and facing the most important decision of his life." He bowed his head and prayed simply,

"Help me, Lord, to know what to say and how to say it to Adam. You've been teaching me patience these past several years, and I may need it now. I need the patience, not with Adam, Father, but with myself. Sometimes I can't keep my thoughts straight and this conversation is really important to me. I know it's important to you, too."

Charles' daughter Sarah, Adam's mother, had called just two nights ago to ask if she and her husband, David, could bring Adam to spend the weekend with his grandparents. She had explained that Adam was at a critical juncture in his life of faith. Apparently, the youth group had just finished a faith-decisions class, and several of Adam's friends were baptized as a result. When Sarah and David had talked to Adam, he expressed uncertainty about why he needed to be baptized since he already lived a Christian life and was a faithful participant in almost every youth activity.

Sarah and David had been hesitant to pressure Adam about baptism; they wanted it to be his decision and not something he did simply to please them. Sarah remembered that her dad had mentioned his work with the Seekers class at his church and had talked about how responsive some of those people had been to his fresh insights on baptism.

"I just thought it might be helpful for him to hear your perspective on these things, Dad," she had commented on the phone. "I just know Adam will listen to you. You guys have always had such a special relationship. Do you mind if we bring him for a visit?"

Charles chuckled to himself at that last question. What grandparent ever minded having a grandchild visit? But this trip would be different, he mused. He had shared his recent experience thinking and teaching about baptism when the kids last visited, but he hadn't been sure anyone was really listening then. Now he needed to get ready for this important visit.

He got up from the porch, put his study materials away, and began to look down the road for a familiar mini-van.

For Discussion

Ask participants to gather in groups of 4 or 5 to answer the following questions, making sure each group is as diverse as possible. Groups should be prepared to share the details of their discussion with the larger class as time permits.

1 Where would you begin the conversation with Adam if you were Charles? Why would you choose this starting point?

2 What are some of the important dimensions of baptism that you would like to share with someone like Adam? How have you come to these understandings? Do they reflect your own experience, your further studies, or your theological reflection on baptism?

3 What would you be careful to avoid in the conversation? Why?

4 How do you determine if a 14-year-old is old enough and mature enough to make a decision as important as this one?

31

5 How would you work with parents like Sarah and David to equip them to deal with their children's important faith decisions?

After gathering the class back together and discussing each group's responses to the above questions, ask the class to answer the following questions either in writing or verbally (these responses may give you insight into areas that need further discussion):

1 What I found most enlightening about our discussion was...

2 What I wish we would talk more about is...

Scenario 2: "A Brother's Love"

The Situation

Sarah Miller hung up the phone and turned to her husband, Roger. "That's interesting," she said. "I just received a phone call from a young man named Willie from the West Coast. We've never met him, but he got our number from his minister. Seems his sister is moving here next week, and he wants us to meet her and help her get unpacked. It's obvious that he loves her very much."

"When will she be here?" Roger asked. "I can get a crew together from our Monday night Bible study."

"Yeah, but that's not all he wants from us," Sarah replied. "This is going to be a unique challenge," she thought. Then smiling, she turned to Roger and told him the details of her conversation with Willie.

Willie had been baptized into Christ just two years earlier and described his time as a disciple as intense and exciting. Like many new converts, he had been anxious to share his new-found faith with all his family and friends. A few had seemed interested but none had chosen to commit themselves to Christ in baptism yet. The closest to making a decision was Willie's sister, Tamika, who was moving to the town where Sarah and Roger served as outreach ministers.

Although frustrated that Tamika would not be where he could talk to her on a regular basis, Willie had been excited to hear about the Miller's ministry. He had planned to call them immediately and encourage them to continue to study with Tamika. He thought an offer to help her unpack might open the door for deeper relationships.

Ironically, one of Tamika's current neighbors, Curt, had been helping her pack and load her truck. As they worked, he had shared his faith in Jesus Christ and soon led Tamika to "accept Jesus into her heart as her personal savior." She had been very excited about making this decision, but Willie had not known how to respond to her news.

Willie simply helped her load her truck and then called the Millers to see if they would set up a study. He wanted his sister to have faith, but he wanted it to be a complete one connecting her deeply to the death, burial and resurrection of Christ. He had been in tears when he ended the conversation with Sarah.

"She'll be here by the end of the week," Sarah told Roger. "Let's get a crew to help her unload and focus our prayers on how we'll proceed in teaching her more about what God desires from her."

For Discussion

Ask participants to gather in groups of 4 or 5 to answer the following questions, making sure each group is as diverse as possible. Groups should be prepared to share the details of their discussion with the larger class as time permits.

1 How many of you have faced dilemmas like this one where a person sincerely committed his or her life to Christ without realizing baptism's connection to his death, burial, and resurrection? What did you find most challenging about this situation? Ask 2 or 3 people to share their experiences.

2 What are some of the important dimensions of baptism that you would like to share with someone

like Tamika? How have you come to these understandings? Do they reflect your own experience, your
further studies, or your reflection on baptism?

3 Where would you begin the conversation with
Tamika if you were Sarah and Roger? Why would
you choose this starting point? What would you be
careful to avoid in your conversation?

4 How would you involve the community of faith in
this situation?

After gathering the class back together and discussing
each group's responses to the above questions, ask the
class to answer the following questions either in writing or verbally (these responses may give you insight
into areas that need further discussion):

1 How has working through this scenario affected your
understanding of baptism?

2 How has your perspective changed or developed as
you've worked through this scenario?

3 How might what you've learned from working
through this scenario affect how you will teach
others about baptism in the future?

Workspace & Notes

Works Cited

Allen, C. Leonard and Danny Gray Swick, *Participating in God's Life: Two Crossroads for Churches of Christ* (Orange, CA; New Leaf Books, 2001): 155–6.

Robert Richardson, *Communings in the Sanctuary*, ed. C. Leonard Allen (Orange, CA: New Leaf Books, 2000): 102.

Alexander Campbell, *The Christian System* (Cincinnati: H.S. Bosworth, 1866): 58.

A.J. Gossip, *From the Edge of the Crowd: Being Musings of a Pagan Mind on Jesus Christ* (Edinburgh: T. & T. Clark, 1924): 230–31.

Martin Luther, *Larg Catechism* 13. In F. Bente and W.H.T. Dau, trans., *The Large Catechism by Martin Luther* (St. Louis: Concordia Publishing House, 1921).

Alexander Campbell, *The Christian System* (Cincinnati: H.S. Bosworth, 1866): 266.

Michael Card, "Scandalon," from album *Scandalon* (Birdwing Music, 1985).

Dietrich Bonhoeffer, *The Cost of Discipleship*, trans. R.H. Fuller, 2nd ed. (New York: Macmillan, 1963): 99.

Dietrich Bonhoeffer, *The Cost of Discipleship*, trans. R.H. Fuller, 2nd ed. (New York: Macmillan, 1963): 46–7.

Robert E. Webber, *Ancient-Future Faith. Rethinking Evangelicalism for a Postmodern World* (Grand Rapids: Baker, 1999): 110.

Jean Vanier, *Community and Growth* (Darton, Longman & Todd, 1979): 10.

Mother Theresa, *A Gift for God: Prayers and Meditations* (New York: Harper & Row, 1975): 19.

Ambrose of Milan, *De Spiritu Sancto*, 1.6.76 (*On the Holy Spirit*). In P. Schaff, et al., eds., *A Select Library of Nicene and Post-Nicene Fathers of the Christian Church*, 2nd series (New York: Christian Literature: 1887–94; reprinted Peabody: Hendrickson, 1994): 10.103.

Carl Braaten, "The Reality of the Resurrection." In Christopher R. Seitz, ed., *Nicene Christianity: The Future for a New Ecumenism* (Grand Rapids: Brazos, 2001): 115.

Thomas Aquinas, *Summa Theologica* 3.66.7. In Fathers of the English Dominican Province, trans., *The Summa Theologica of St. Thomas Aquinas*, 2nd ed. (1920). Online edition copyright 2001. <http://www.newadvent.org/summa>.

Looking for more? Check out the other books in the *Heart of the Restoration* series!

The Crux of the Matter: Crisis, Tradition, & the Future of Churches of Christ

by Jeff Childers, Doug Foster, & Jack Reese

"Perhaps the most important book in Churches of Christ for the last decade."

Gary Holloway, Lipscomb University

ACU Press · ISBN 0-89112-036-X · trade paperback · $14.95

God's Holy Fire: The Nature & Function of Scripture

by Ken Cukrowski, Mark Hamilton, & James Thompson

"This book is a careful, intelligent, and gentle call for Christians once again to 'take up and read.' Well aware of their audience, the authors provide a clear orientation to the literary and historical tools needed to read the Bible for understanding.

David Fleer, Rochester College

ACU Press · ISBN 0-89112-037-8 · trade paperback · $14.95

Unveiling Glory: Visions of Christ's Transforming Presence

by Jeff Childers & Frederick Aquino

"In a religious milieu where great heat is often generated over the minute and peripheral, it is wonderful to read a book reminding us that the only legitimate and life-giving heat radiates from the Son at the center. *Unveiling Glory* sits us in front of Jesus and allows us to warm ourselves in his glow."

Tim Woodroof, Otter Creek Church of Christ

ACU Press · ISBN 0-89112-038-6 · trade paperback · $14.95

Find us on the web at www.acu.edu/acupress

or write to us at ACU Press; ACU Box 29138; Abilene TX 79699-9138